montessori

Spanish

workbook

A Montessori Spanish Book for 3+ Years Old:
Learn Reading, Numbers, Science, Geography and Music.
For Home Learning, School and Travel

by Julia Palmarola

For my daughters:
"mi luna y mi estrella."

TABLE OF CONTENTS

1. Learn Spanish with Montessori!
2. Introduction to the Spanish language
3. La familia - *Family*
4. Comer y beber – *Eating and drinking*
5. Poner la mesa – *Setting the table*
6. Matemáticas y números – *Math and numbers*
7. Las partes del cuerpo – *Parts of the body*
8. Ciencia y naturaleza: animales – *Science and nature: animals*
9. Geografía - *Geography*
10. Música - *Music*

Learn Spanish with Montessori!

{ Introduction for parents and caregivers }

The teaching of a second language must begin, ideally, at the time of birth. It's never *too soon* to start! This interactive workbook will help young children to learn Spanish with activities based on the **Montessori Method**. It contains cut-outs, three-part cards, and many other materials based on touching and handling cards, reading, writing, matching, coloring, etc. Children will be able to work independently or under the guidance of an adult, depending on their age and previous knowledge.

What is the Montessori method?

The Montessori method is a teaching system devised by Maria Montessori, an Italian scientist and pedagogue who created a revolutionary learning system in the early twentieth century. It fosters the independence of children and their ability to absorb knowledge *like sponges*. The only condition for them to do so is to provide them with a rich and stimulating environment where they are given freedom to investigate.

If you wish to know more about the Montessori method and how to use it, I encourage you to read my other book, the ***Practical Guide to the Montessori Method at Home*** (Julia Palmarola, 2018) and the other two related titles: ***Montessori Reading Workbook*** and ***Montessori Math Workbook***, by the same author.

Using three-part cards

Three-part cards, like the ones above these lines, help children learn new words intuitively. The first card is already printed on each page. The child must cut out the matching cards (found on the following pages) and paste them or place them in the right place. Keep the cards in an envelope if you want to repeat this activity later!

Introduction
to the Spanish Language

Young children have a remarkable capacity to absorb new information, which is why introducing languages at an early age can be much easier and immensely beneficial. By engaging in language learning activities from early childhood, children not only develop essential linguistic skills but also cultivate cultural awareness and cognitive flexibility. This workbook can be used by children from the age of 3 on, and it aims to provide fun and interactive activities to explore the Spanish language while learning useful concepts that will encourage their overall cognitive development.

Introduction to Sounds
and Basic Pronunciation in Spanish

Vowels: Spanish has five vowels (a, e, i, o, and u), and they are pronounced consistently. Unlike in English, each vowel generally has only one sound. Practice saying these vowels clearly and distinctly.

- "a" is pronounced like the "a" in "father."
- "e" is pronounced like the "e" in "get."
- "i" is pronounced like the "ee" in "see."
- "o" is pronounced like the "o" in "go."
- "u" is pronounced like the "oo" in "boot."

Consonants: Most consonants in Spanish have similar sounds to English. However, there are a few differences to keep in mind. For example, the letter "c" before "e" or "i" is pronounced like the "th" in "thin." The letter "j" is pronounced like the "h" in "hat," but with a raspy sound from the back of your throat.

Rolling "R": Spanish has a rolled or trilled "r" sound, which can be challenging for English speakers. To practice, place your tongue against the roof of your mouth, just behind your front teeth, and create a vibrating sound by blowing air.

Here's a step-by-step guide to help you pronounce the Spanish "r" properly:

- Place the tip of your tongue against the roof of your mouth, just behind your front teeth.
- Relax your tongue and create a slight space for the air to pass through.
- Make a gentle vibrating or rolling sound with your tongue as the air passes through the space. This creates the distinct "rr" sound in Spanish.

Here are a few words to get you started:

- "Perro" (dog)
- "Rápido" (fast)
- "Rosa" (rose)

Stress and Syllables: In Spanish, the stress is usually on the second-to-last syllable of a word. Pay attention to where the stress falls and emphasize that syllable when speaking.

Other ideas to teach Spanish to your children

- Allow your child to watch cartoons only in Spanish;
- If you have the possibility, enrol your child in a bilingual school or playgroup;
- Check for expat associations in your area and ask for permission to join them. In many cities, there are expatriate mother groups who meet regularly on playdates. You might also find some of these groups through social networks. In many cases, they will accept native mothers and children, as long as they are respectful with their culture and make an effort to speak their language.
- If you don't speak Spanish yourself, look for a bilingual or foreign baby sitter or get an au-pair.

Mi familia

My family

¡Hola!

Hello!

Me llamo Sofía.

My name is Sofía.

mamá   papá

bebé

hijo

Sofía

hija

Esta es la familia de Sofía.

This is Sofía's family.

madre

Paste the matching picture here.

Paste the matching word here.

padre

Paste the matching picture here.

Paste the matching word here.

hija

Paste the matching picture here.

Paste the matching word here.

hijo

Paste the matching picture here.

Paste the matching word here.

bebé

Paste the matching picture here.

Paste the matching word here.

abuela

Paste the matching picture here.

Paste the matching word here.

Yo soy Sofía.

I am Sofía.

Sofía has a brother and a sister.

Sofía tiene un hermano y una hermana.

Sofía tiene un hermano y una hermana.

Sofia's mother is called Martina.

La madre de Sofía se llama Martina.

La madre de Sofía se llama Martina.

Sofia's father is called Luis.

El padre de Sofía se llama Luis.

El padre de Sofía se llama Luis.

abuela

madre

hijo

bebé

padre	hija

madre	primo	abuelo
padre	prima	abuela
hijo	sobrino	tío
hija	sobrina	tía

La familia.

Paste the right word.

Check the back of this page to see the right answers.

mother

father

son

daughter

cousin (he)

cousin (she)

La familia.

mother | madre

father | padre

son | hijo

daughter | hija

cousin (he) | primo

cousin (she) | prima

La familia.

Paste the right word.

Check the back of this page to see the right answers.

nephew

niece

grandfather

grandmother

uncle

aunt

La familia.

nephew | sobrino

niece | sobrina

grandfather | abuelo

grandmother | abuela

uncle | tío

aunt | tía

Comer y beber.

Eating and drinking.

Me gustan
las manzanas.

Me gustan las manzanas.

I like apples.

comer

to eat

beber

to drink

Sofía eats cheese.

Sofía come queso.

Sofía come queso.

Sofía eats broccoli.

Sofía come brócoli.

Sofía come brócoli.

Sofía drinks milk.

Sofía bebe leche.

Sofía bebe leche.

Sofía drinks water.

Sofía bebe agua.

Sofía bebe agua.

manzana

Paste the matching picture here.

Paste the matching word here.

naranja

Paste the matching picture here.

Paste the matching word here.

queso

Paste the matching picture here.

Paste the matching word here.

zanahoria

Paste the matching picture here.

Paste the matching word here.

tomate

Paste the matching picture here.

Paste the matching word here.

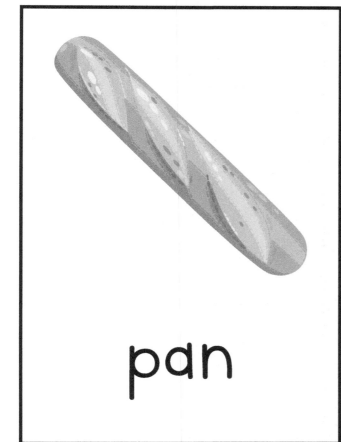

pan

Paste the matching picture here.

Paste the matching word here.

huevo

Paste the matching picture here.

Paste the matching word here.

uva

Paste the matching picture here.

Paste the matching word here.

pescado

Paste the matching picture here.

Paste the matching word here.

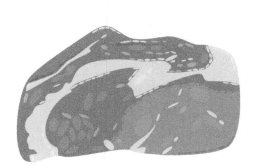

carne

Paste the matching picture here.

Paste the matching word here.

piña

Paste the matching picture here.

Paste the matching word here.

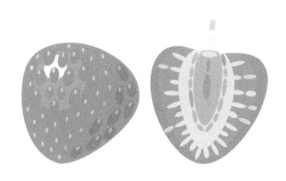

fresa

Paste the matching picture here.

Paste the matching word here.

sopa

Paste the matching picture here.

Paste the matching word here.

ensalada

Paste the matching picture here.

Paste the matching word here.

helado

Paste the matching picture here.

Paste the matching word here.

leche

Paste the matching picture here.

Paste the matching word here.

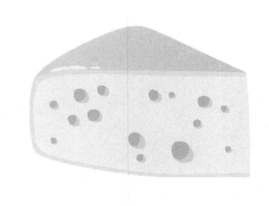

queso

manzana

naranja

zanahoria

pan

tomate

uva

huevo

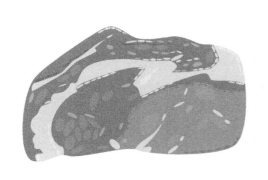

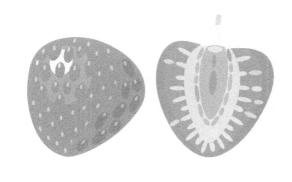

pescado

fresa

carne

piña

 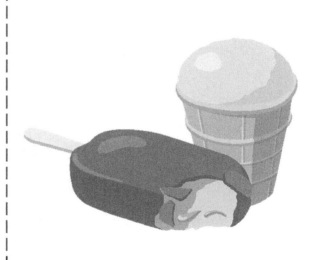

helado

leche

sopa

ensalada

fruta
fruits

verdura
vegetables

piña

fresa

berenjena

pimiento

zanahoria

brócoli

naranja

manzana

fruta
fruits

verdura
vegetables

piña

fresa

pimiento

brócoli

manzana

naranja

zanahoria

berenjena

Poner la mesa
Setting the table

tenedor cucharilla cuchillo

vaso servilleta cuchara plato

Poner la mesa
Setting the table

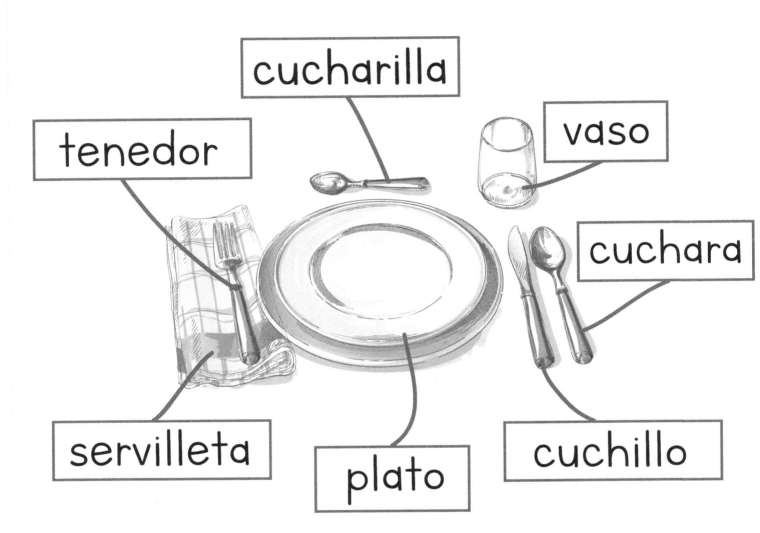

cucharilla

vaso

tenedor

cuchara

servilleta

plato

cuchillo

La comida - Food

Paste the right word.

Check the back of this page to see the right answers.

tomato

egg

carrot

soup

orange

tomate   sopa   naranja

huevo   zanahoria

La comida - Food

Answer key

tomato | **tomate**

egg | **huevo**

carrot | **zanahoria**

soup | **sopa**

orange | **naranja**

La comida - Food

Paste the right word.

Check the back of this page to see the right answers.

cheese [ ]

apple [ ]

milk [ ]

salad [ ]

ice cream [ ]

leche

queso

helado

ensalada

manzana

La comida - Food

Answer key

cheese | queso

apple | manzana

milk | leche

salad | ensalada

ice cream | helado

Los números y contar
Numbers and counting

7

Sofía

I am seven years old.

Tengo siete años

Tengo siete años

10

Manuel

My brother is ten years old.

Mi hermano tiene diez años.

Mi hermano tiene diez años.

Numbers and counting

3

Paula

Paula is three years old.

Paula tiene tres años

Paula tiene tres años

1

Martina

Martina is one year old.

Martina tiene un año.

Martina tiene un año.

How old are you?

¿Cuántos años tienes?

Números del 1 al 12

1 — uno

2 — dos

3 — tres

4 — cuatro

5 — cinco

6 — seis

Números del 1 al 12

7   siete

8   ocho

9   nueve

10   diez

11   once

12   doce

Los números – Numbers

Paste the missing letter.
Check the back of this page to see the right answers.

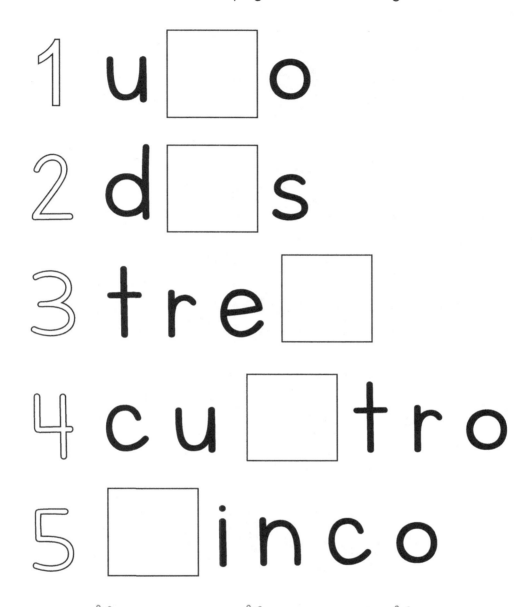

1 u☐o

2 d☐s

3 tre☐

4 cu☐tro

5 ☐inco

- - - ✂ - - - - - ✂ - - - - - ✂ - - - - - ✂ - - - - - ✂ - - -

c   n   s

o   q

Los números – Numbers

1 u n o

2 d o s

3 t r e s

4 c u a t r o

5 c i n c o

Las partes del cuerpo
Parts of the body

El cuerpo
The body

Los músculos
The muscles

Los huesos
The bones

Los órganos
The organs

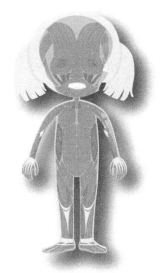

Muscles help us move.

Los músculos nos ayudan a movernos

The skeleton is the internal structure of our body.

El esqueleto es la estructura interna
de nuestro cuerpo

The heart and lungs are organs.

El corazón y los pulmones son órganos.

Las partes del cuerpo
Parts of the body

pie | boca | pelo | rodilla

mano | nariz | pierna

brazo | oreja | ojo

Las partes del cuerpo
Parts of the body

pelo

nariz

ojo

oreja

boca

brazo

mano

rodilla

pierna

pie

Ciencia y naturaleza
Science and nature

Animales

Los animales son seres vivos.
Animals are living beings.

Animales domésticos

Domestic animals

perro

pájaro

pez

gato

¿Tienes una mascota?

Do you have a pet?

Sí ☐   No ☐

Yes.   No.

gato

Paste the matching picture here.

Paste the matching word here.

perro

Paste the matching picture here.

Paste the matching word here.

conejo

Paste the matching picture here.

Paste the matching word here.

periquito

Paste the matching picture here.

Paste the matching word here.

loro

Paste the matching picture here.

Paste the matching word here.

pez

Paste the matching picture here.

Paste the matching word here.

tortuga

Paste the matching picture here.

Paste the matching word here.

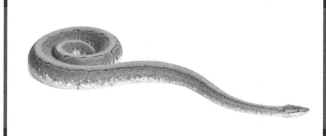

serpiente

Paste the matching picture here.

Paste the matching word here.

camaleón

Paste the matching picture here.

Paste the matching word here.

araña

Paste the matching picture here.

Paste the matching word here.

cerdo

Paste the matching picture here.

Paste the matching word here.

ratón

Paste the matching picture here.

Paste the matching word here.

burro

Paste the matching picture here.

Paste the matching word here.

vaca

Paste the matching picture here.

Paste the matching word here.

caballo

Paste the matching picture here.

Paste the matching word here.

oveja

Paste the matching picture here.

Paste the matching word here.

gato

perro

conejo

periquito

pez

loro

serpiente

tortuga

camaleón

araña

cerdo

ratón

caballo

burro

vaca

oveja

Mamíferos	Aves	Reptiles
Mammals	Birds	Reptiles

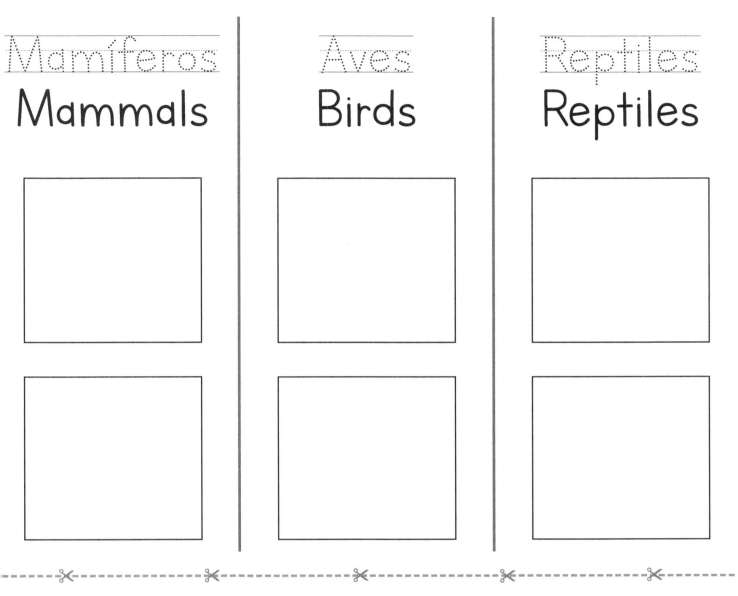

pato

camaleón

gato

lagarto

gallo

perro

Mamíferos	Aves	Reptiles
Mammals	Birds	Reptiles

perro

pato

camaleón

gato

gallo

lagarto

Mamíferos	Aves	Reptiles
Mammals	Birds	Reptiles

loro

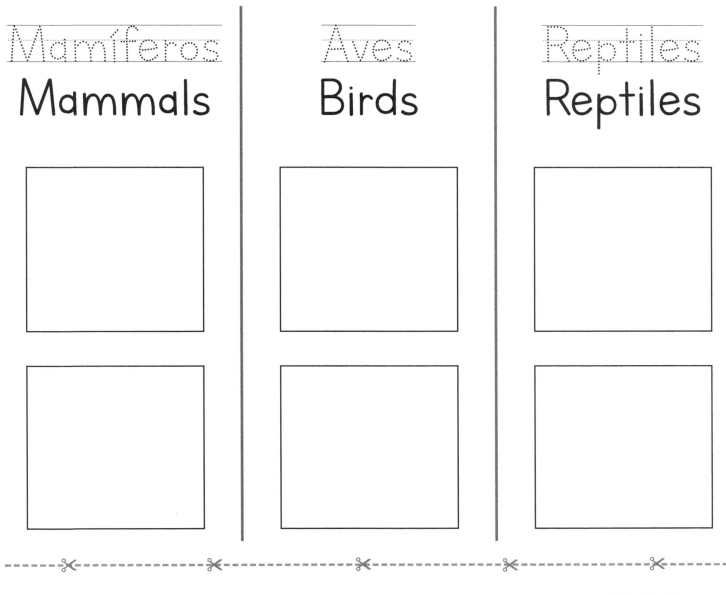

caballo

periquito

tortuga

serpiente

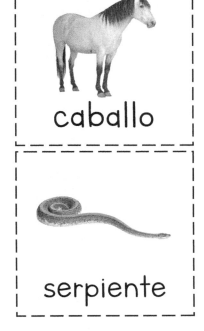

cerdo

Mamíferos	Aves	Reptiles
Mammals	Birds	Reptiles

caballo

loro

tortuga

cerdo

periquito

serpiente

Geografía
Geography

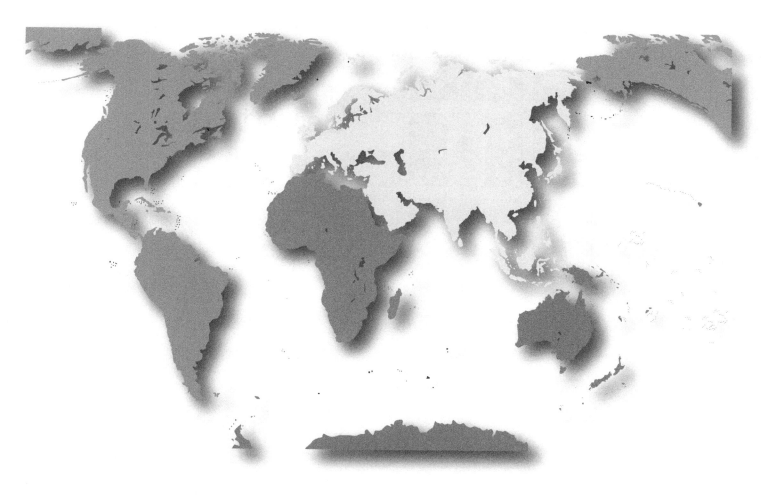

El mundo
The world

Geografía
Geography

Países
Countries

Banderas
Flags

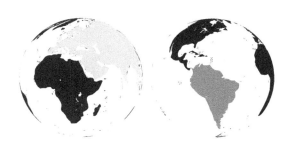

Continentes
Continents

Europa

Paste the matching picture here.

Paste the matching word here.

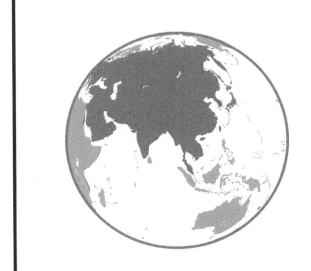

Asia

Paste the matching picture here.

Paste the matching word here.

África

Paste the matching picture here.

Paste the matching word here.

América del Sur

Paste the matching picture here.

Paste the matching word here.

Oceanía

Paste the matching picture here.

Paste the matching word here.

América del Norte

Paste the matching picture here.

Paste the matching word here.

España

Paste the matching picture here.

Paste the matching word here.

Reino Unido

Paste the matching picture here.

Paste the matching word here.

México

Paste the matching picture here.

Paste the matching word here.

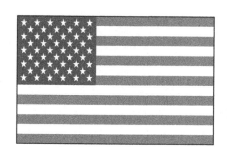

Estados Unidos

Paste the matching picture here.

Paste the matching word here.

Argentina

Paste the matching picture here.

Paste the matching word here.

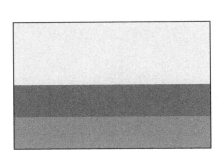

Colombia

Paste the matching picture here.

Paste the matching word here.

Europa

América del Sur

Asia

África

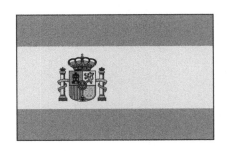

Oceanía

Reino Unido

América del Norte

España

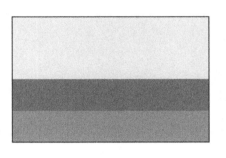

México

Argentina

Estados Unidos

Colombia

¿Dónde vives?

Where do you live?

I live in Spain.

Yo vivo en España.

Yo vivo en España.

My mother is from Mexico.

Mi madre es de México.

Mi madre es de México.

Where are you from?

¿De dónde eres?

Paula

Paula lives in Colombia.

Paula vive en Colombia.

Paula vive en Colombia.

Oliver

Oliver is from the United States.

Oliver es de los Estados Unidos.

Oliver es de los Estados Unidos.

William

William travels to Argentina.

William viaja a Argentina.

William viaja a Argentina.

La música

Music

Los instrumentos musicales

Musical instruments

Instrumentos musicales
Musical instruments

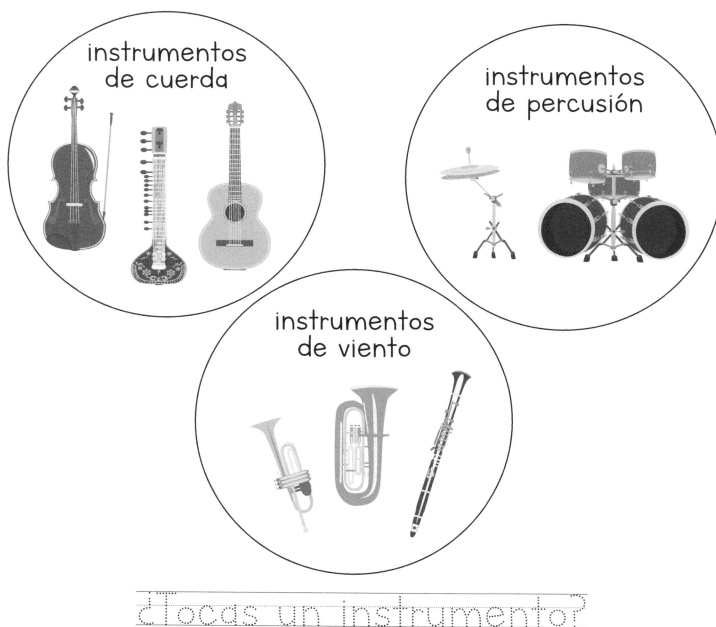

instrumentos
de cuerda

instrumentos
de percusión

instrumentos
de viento

¿Tocas un instrumento?

Do you play an instrument?

 Sí. ☐   No. ☐

Yes.   No.

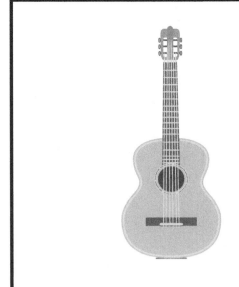

guitarra

Paste the matching picture here.

Paste the matching word here.

piano

Paste the matching picture here.

Paste the matching word here.

violín

Paste the matching picture here.

Paste the matching word here.

trompeta

Paste the matching picture here.

Paste the matching word here.

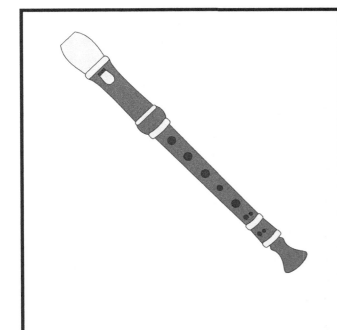

flauta

Paste the matching picture here.

Paste the matching word here.

tambor

Paste the matching picture here.

Paste the matching word here.

saxofón

Paste the matching picture here.

Paste the matching word here.

maracas

Paste the matching picture here.

Paste the matching word here.

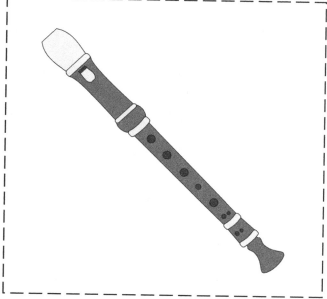

flauta

tambor

maracas

saxofón

violín

guitarra

piano

trompeta

Los instrumentos musicales

Paste the missing letter.
Check the back of this page to see the right answers.

Los instrumentos musicales

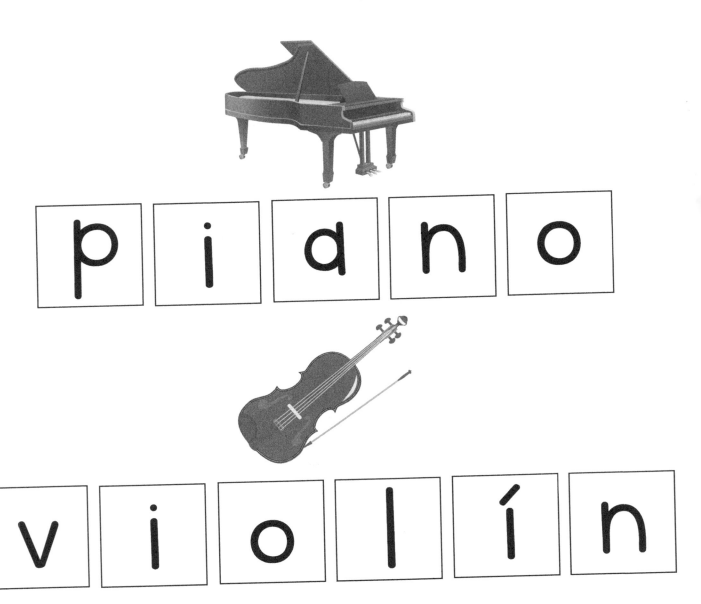

p i a n o

v i o l í n

¡Yo hablo español!

I speak Spanish!

¡Adiós!

Goodbye!

Mis notas:

Mis notas:

Other books you might like:

Practical Guide to the Montessori Method at Home

Julia Palmarola is a Montessori author and supporter of respectful parenting techniques, homeschooling and alternative teaching methods.

She is the author of the **Practical Guide to the Montessori Method at Home** (Julia Palmarola, 2018), a best-selling manual sold in eleven countries and translated to four languages. This book is aimed at parents who want to apply the Montessori Method in a home environment. It includes more than one hundred easy and low budget activity ideas. This book is also available on audiobook format.

Montessori Reading Workbook

A learn to read activity book with Montessori reading tools.
Available in English, Spanish, German and Italian.

Montessori Math Workbook

Learn numbers, counting, addition and subtraction.
Available in English, Spanish, German and Italian.

Made in the USA
Middletown, DE
22 June 2023

33249279R00064